DEEP
BLUE SEA
COLORING BOOK For SENIORS

ISBN-13: 978-1523872718
ISBN-10: 1523872713

2nd Printing

Published by: Argon Media, LLC
1026 28th ST Box 9926
Wyoming, MI 49519

THIS PAGE IS INTENTIONALLY LEFT BLANK AS A BLEED THROUGH PAGE TO PREVENT INK FROM DAMAGING YOUR ARTWORK. ☺

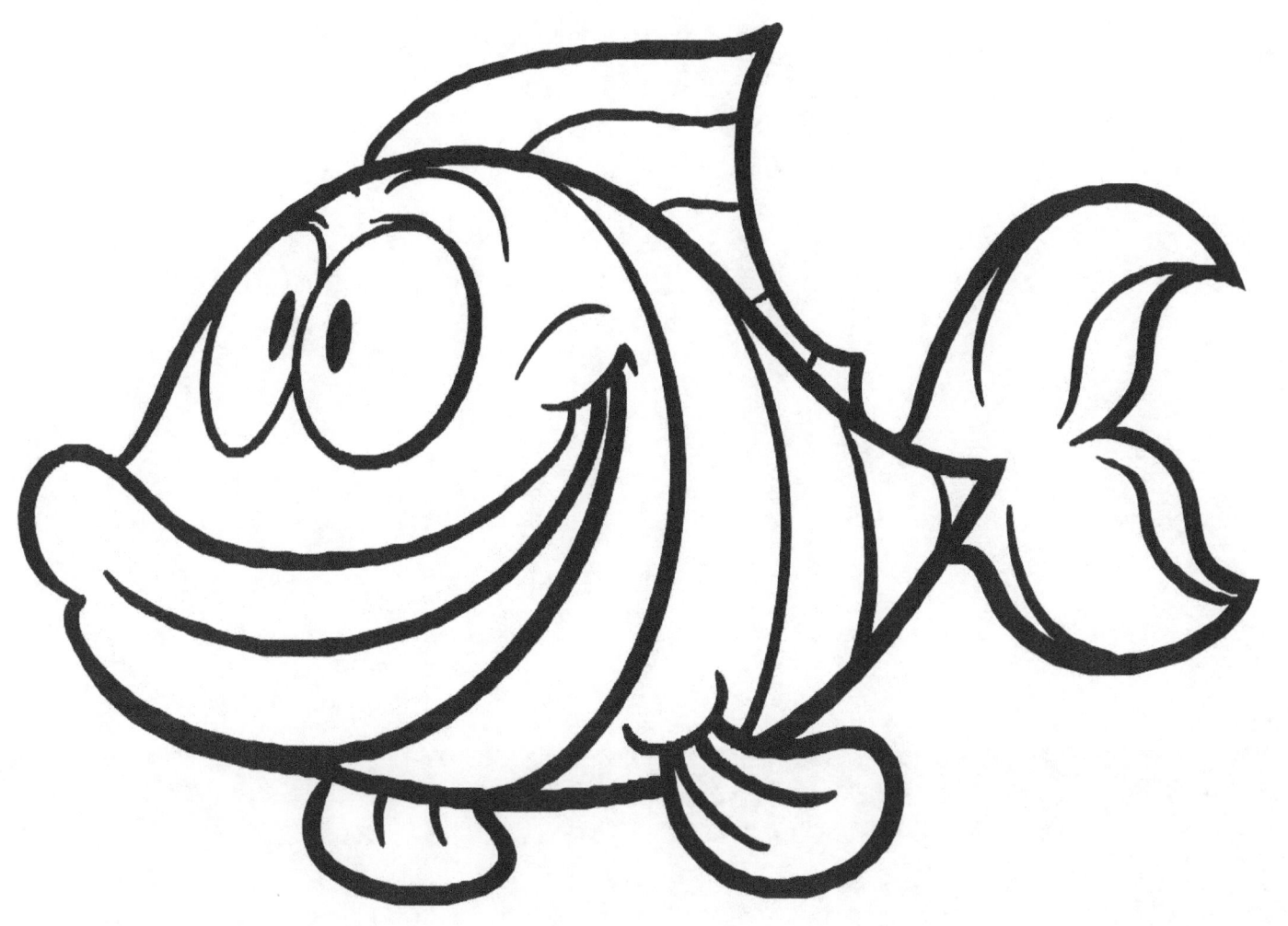

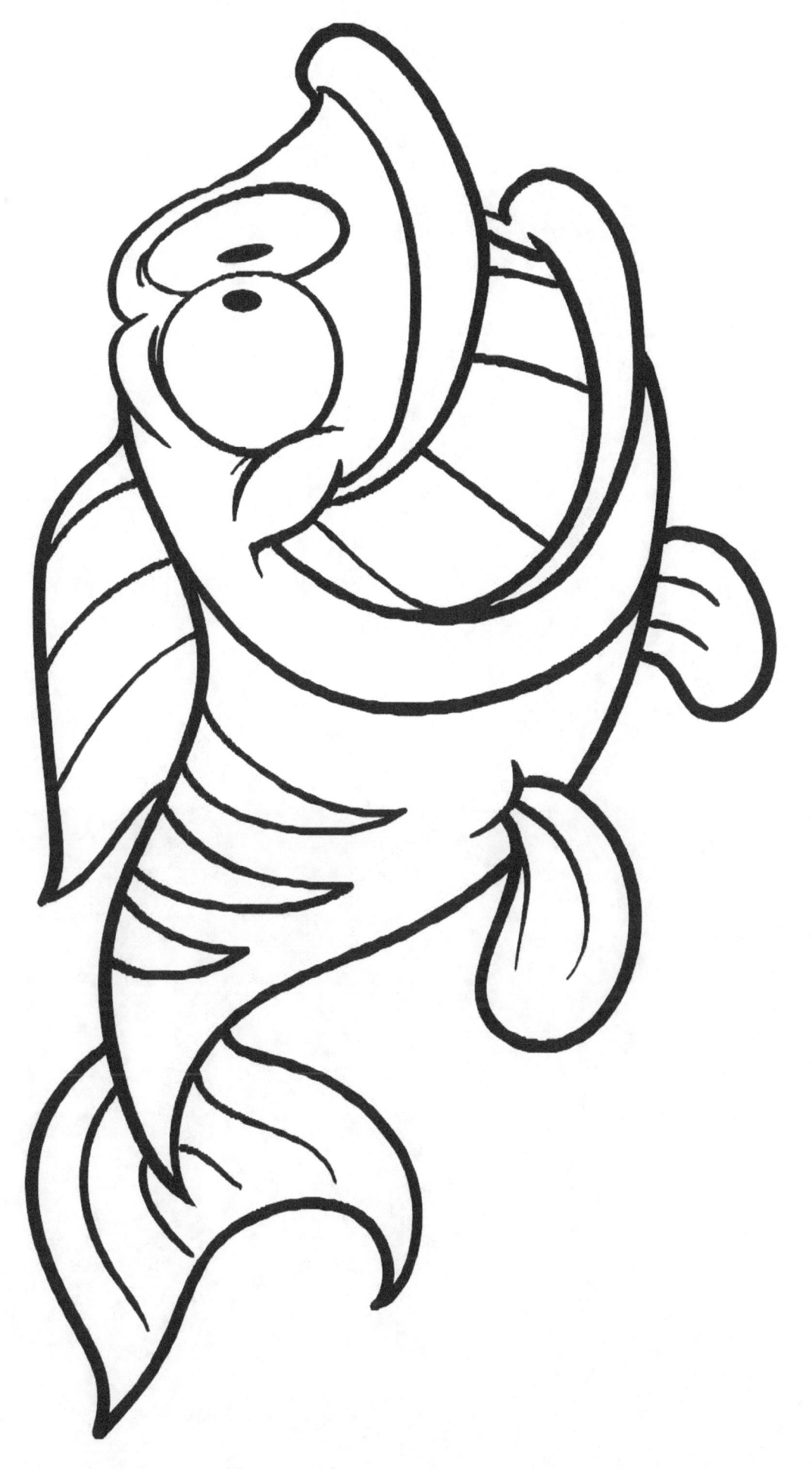

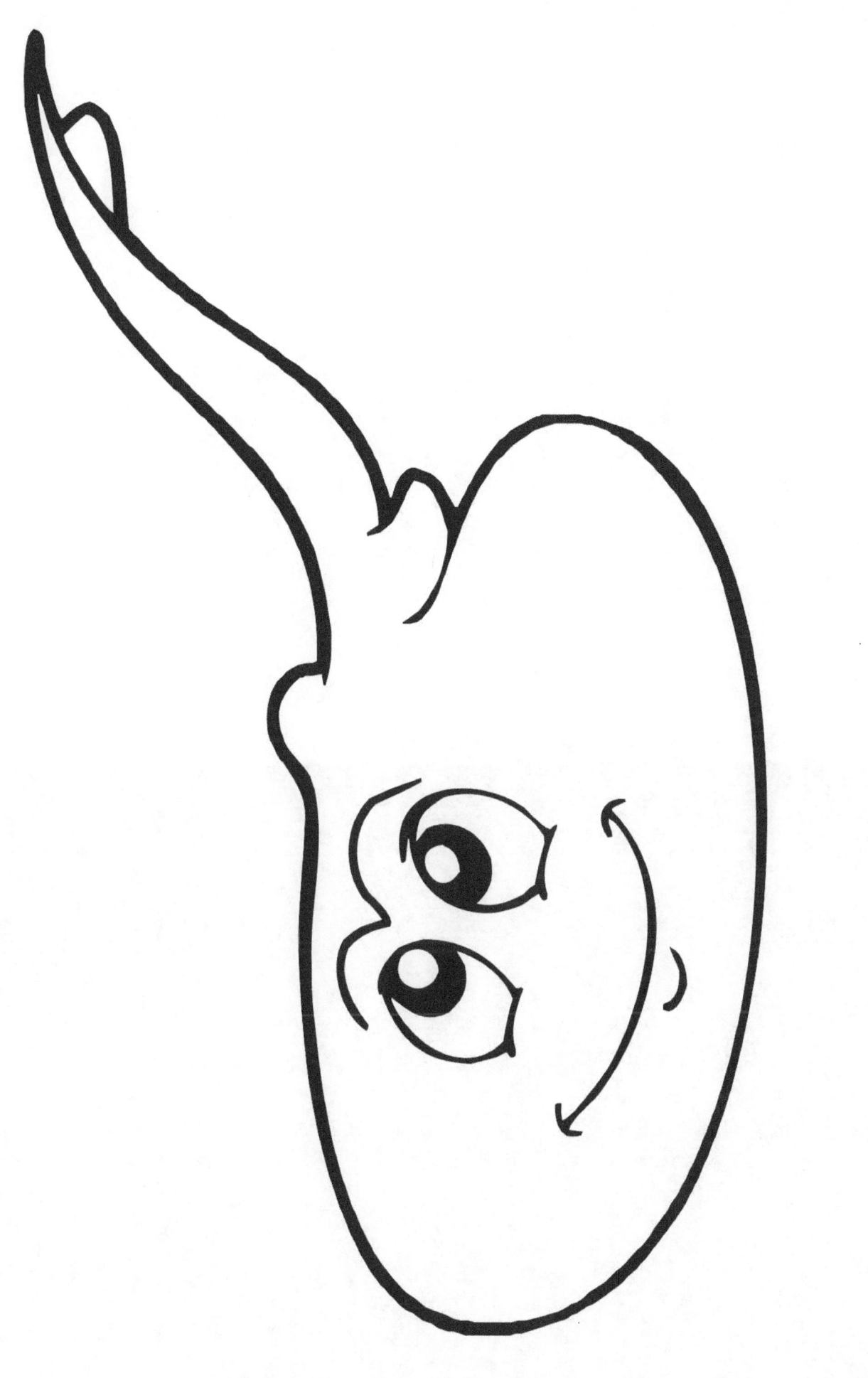

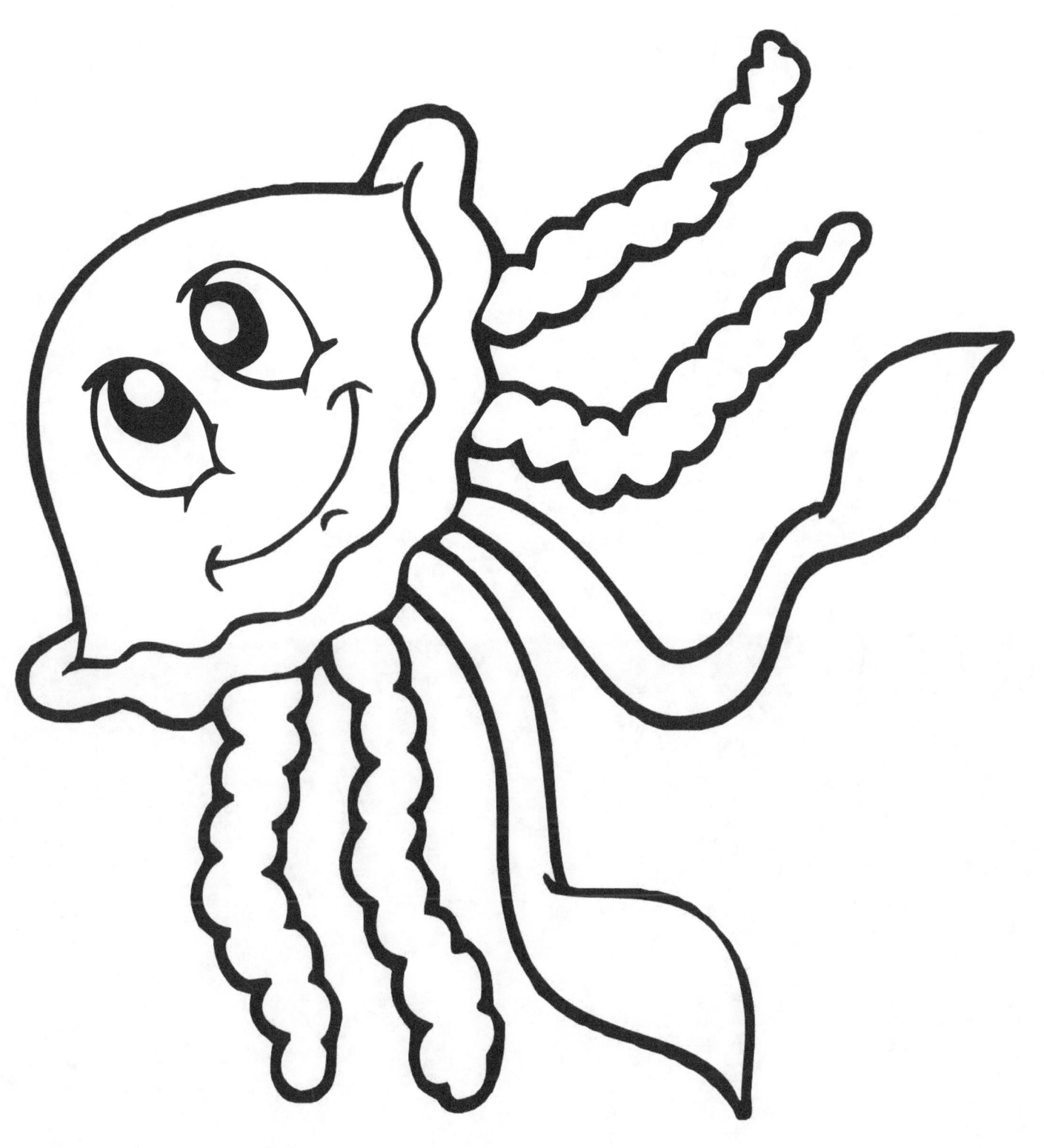

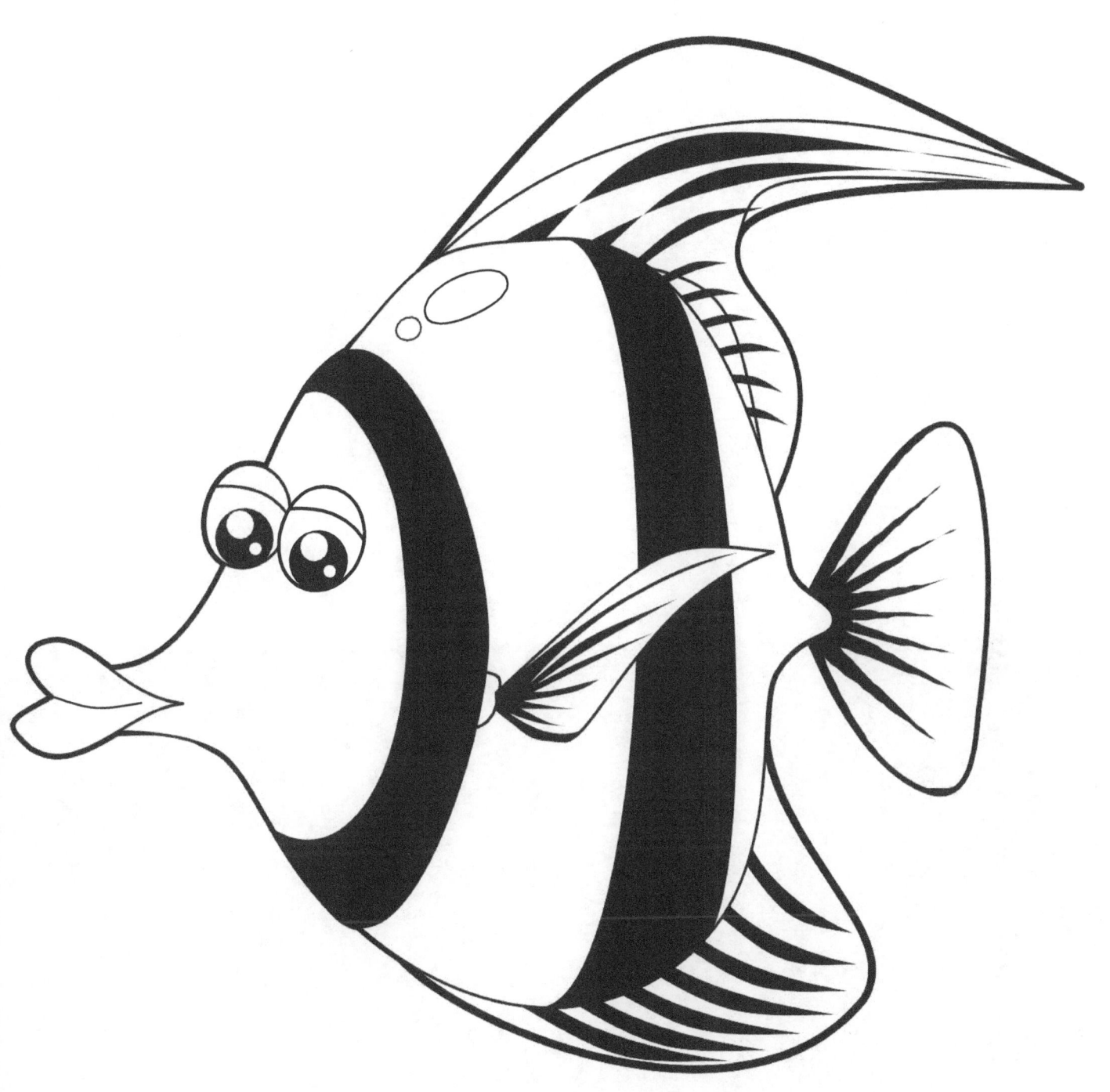

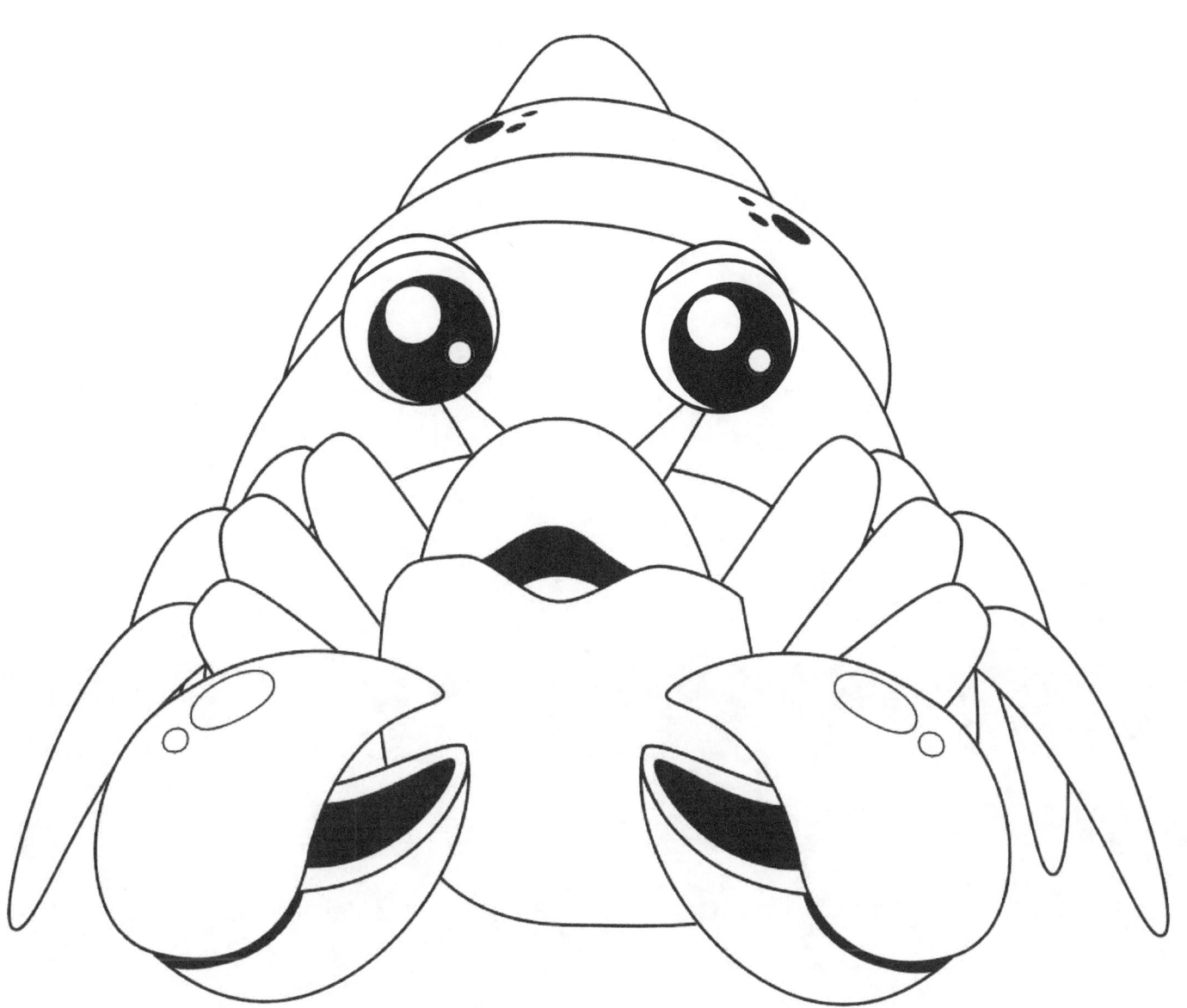

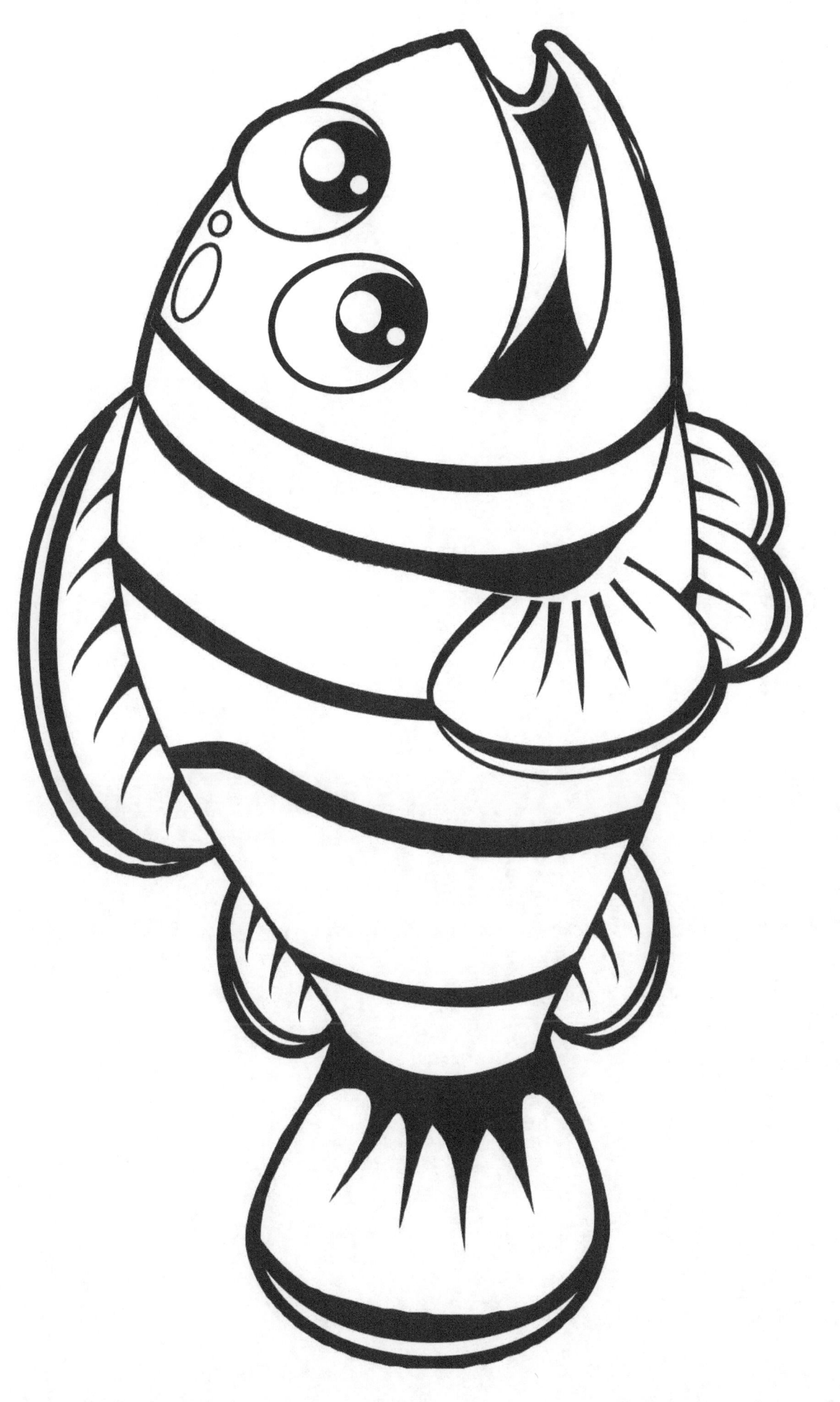

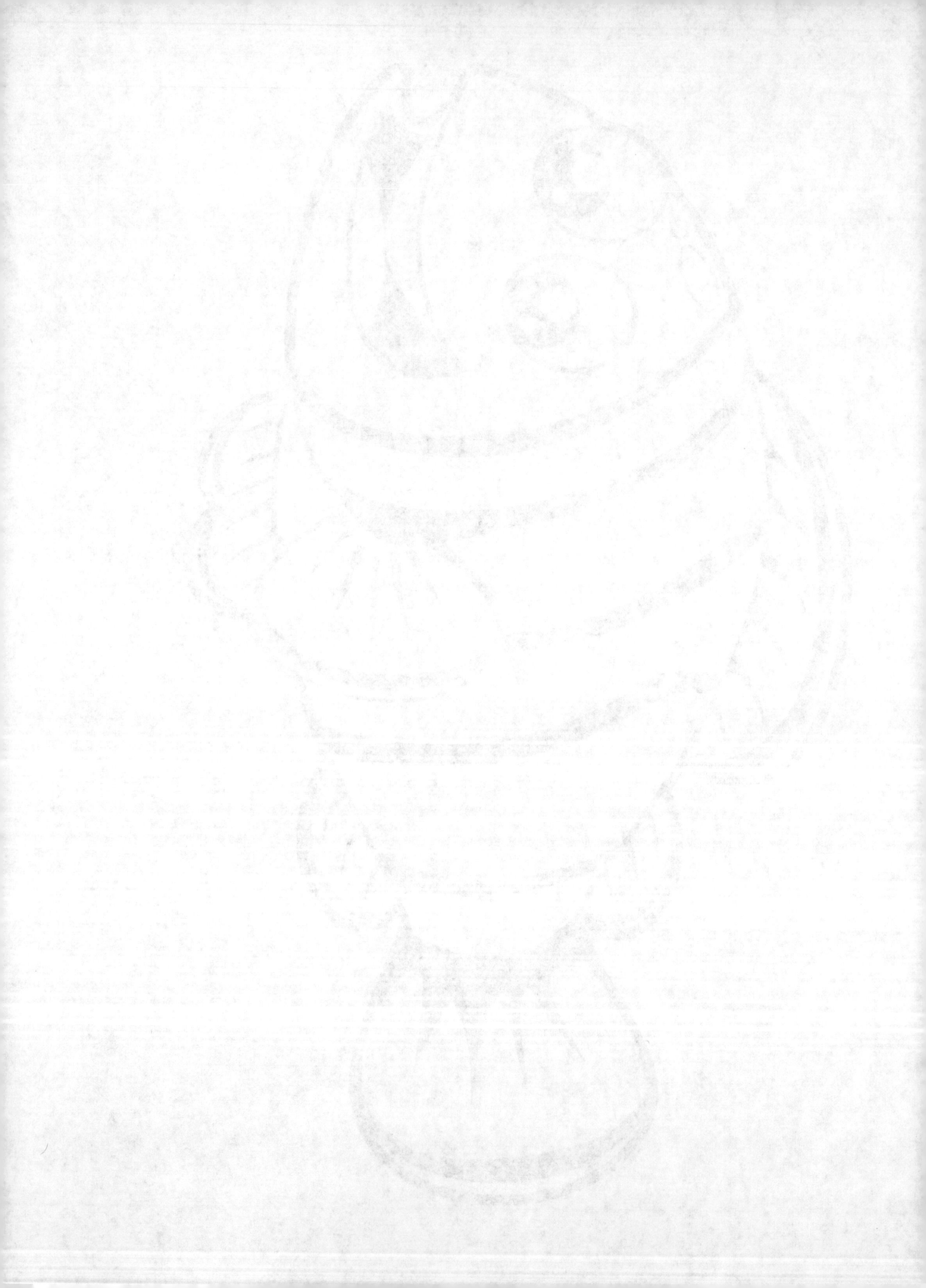

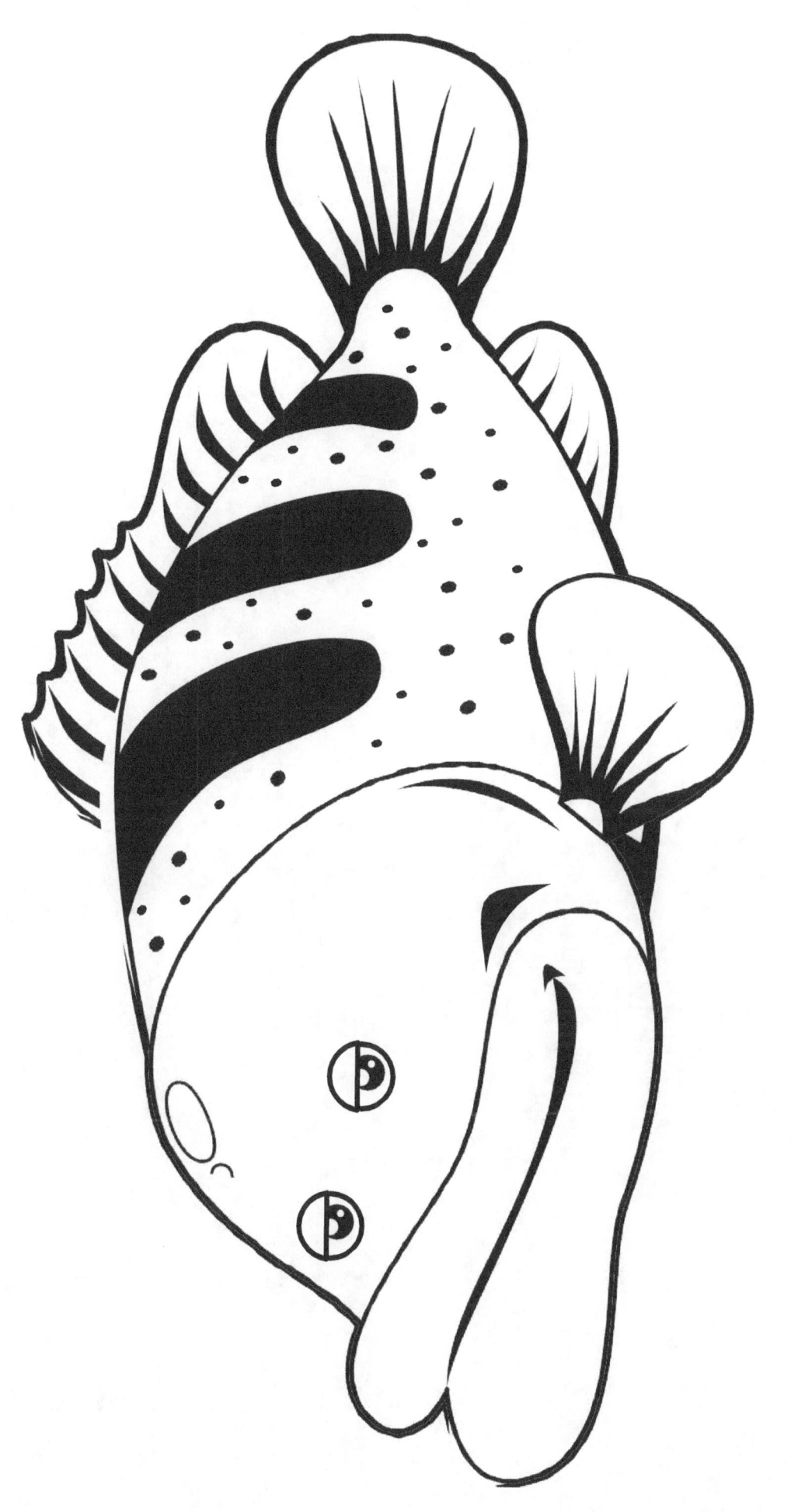

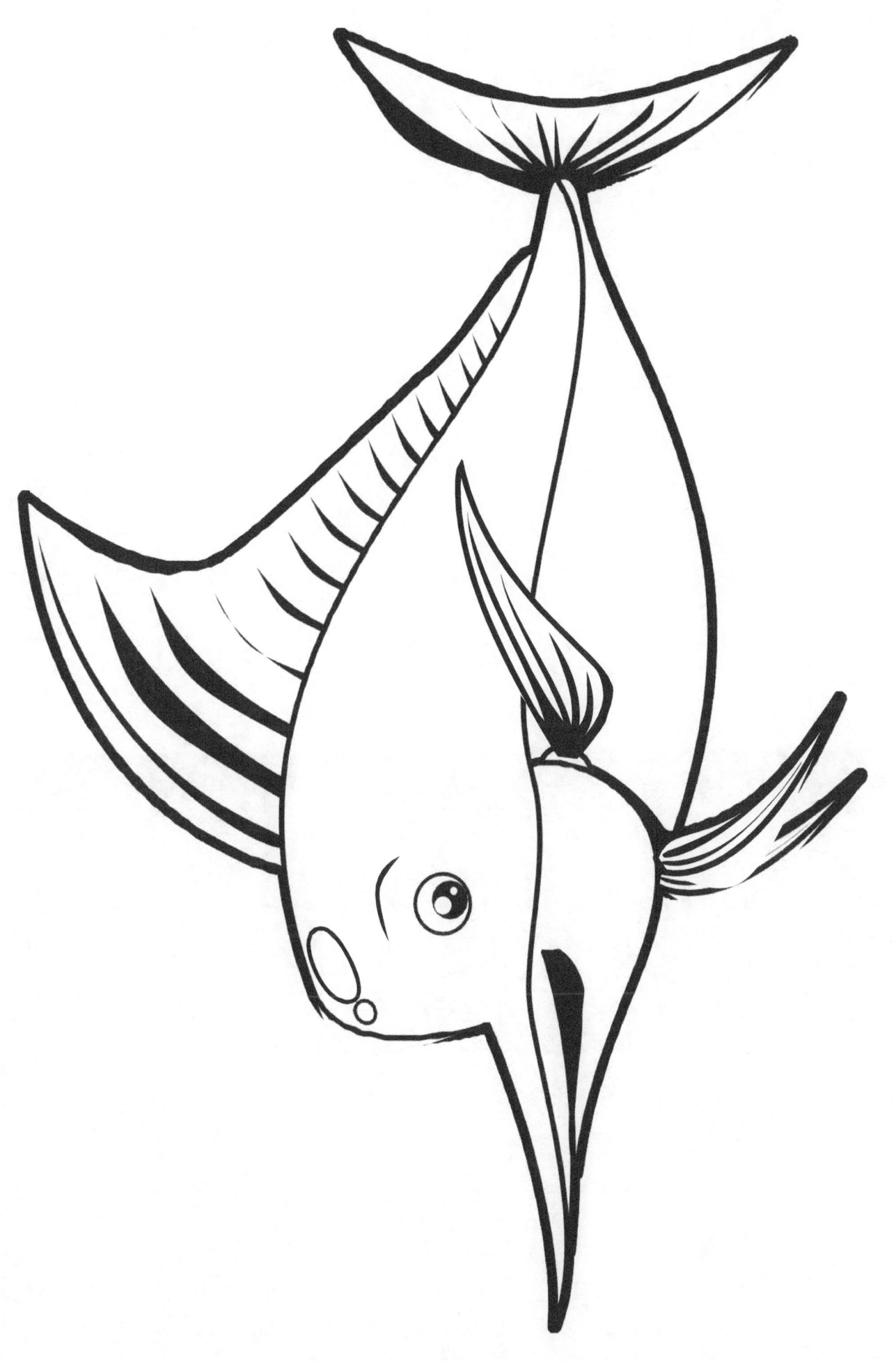

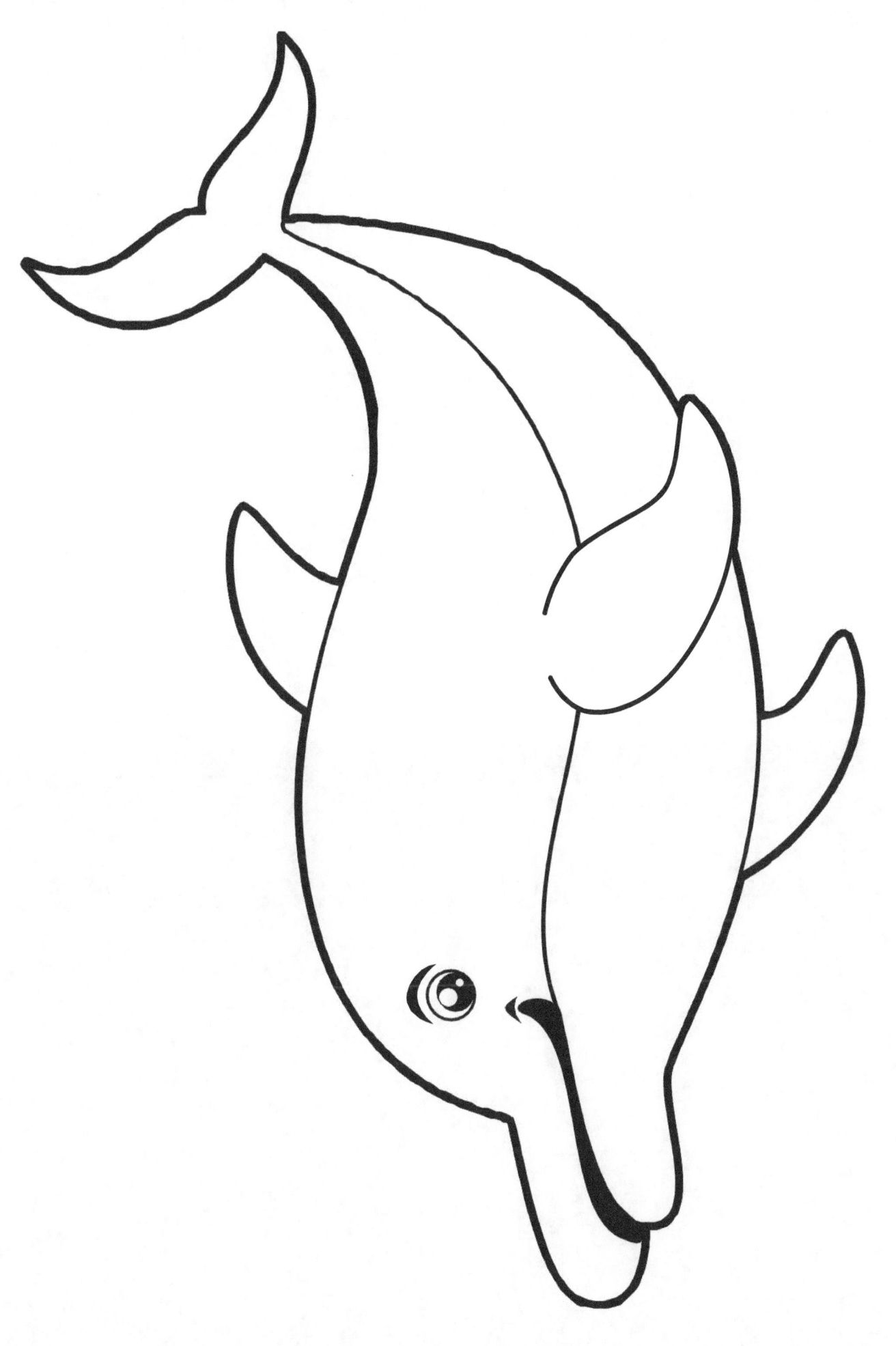

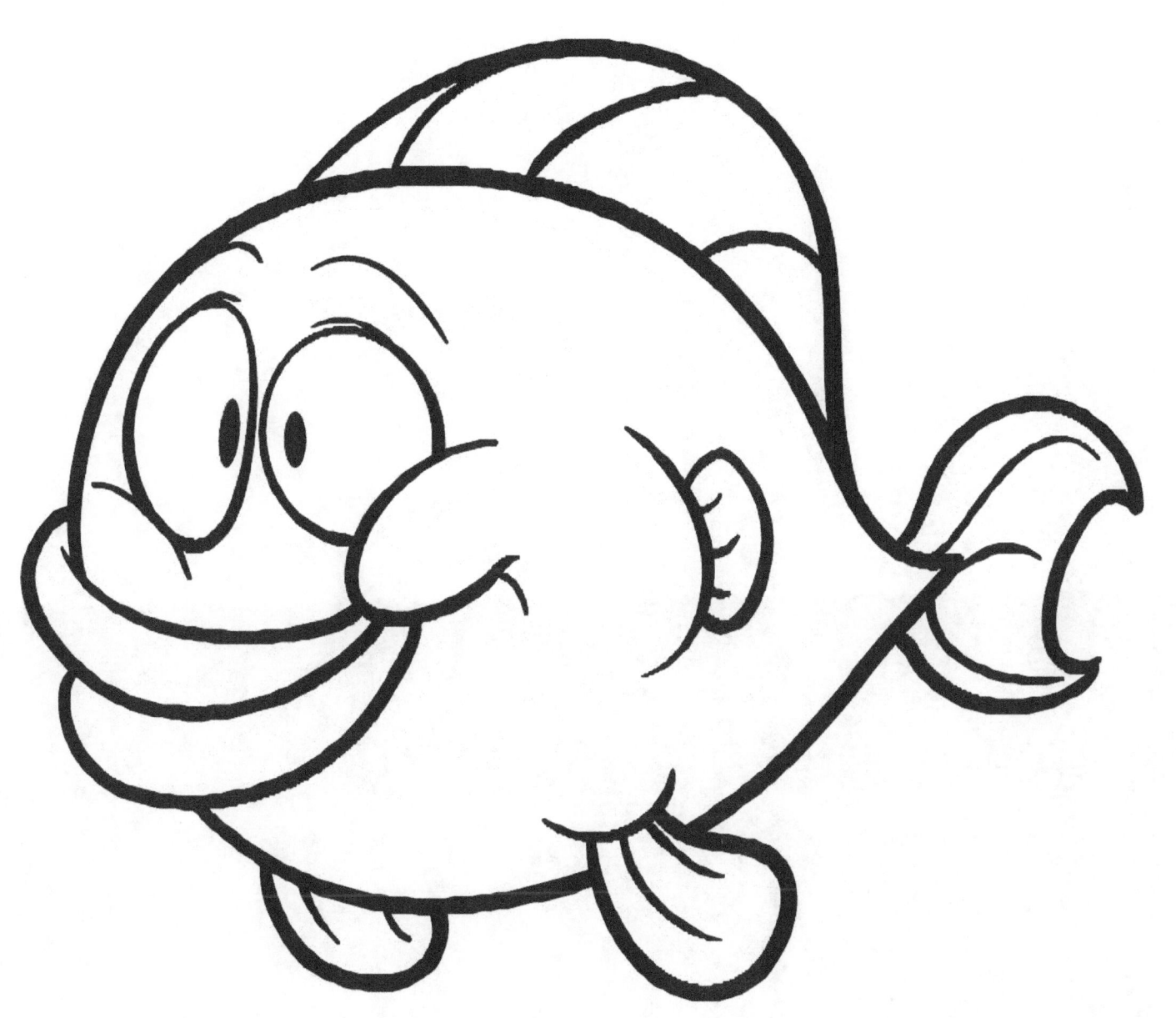

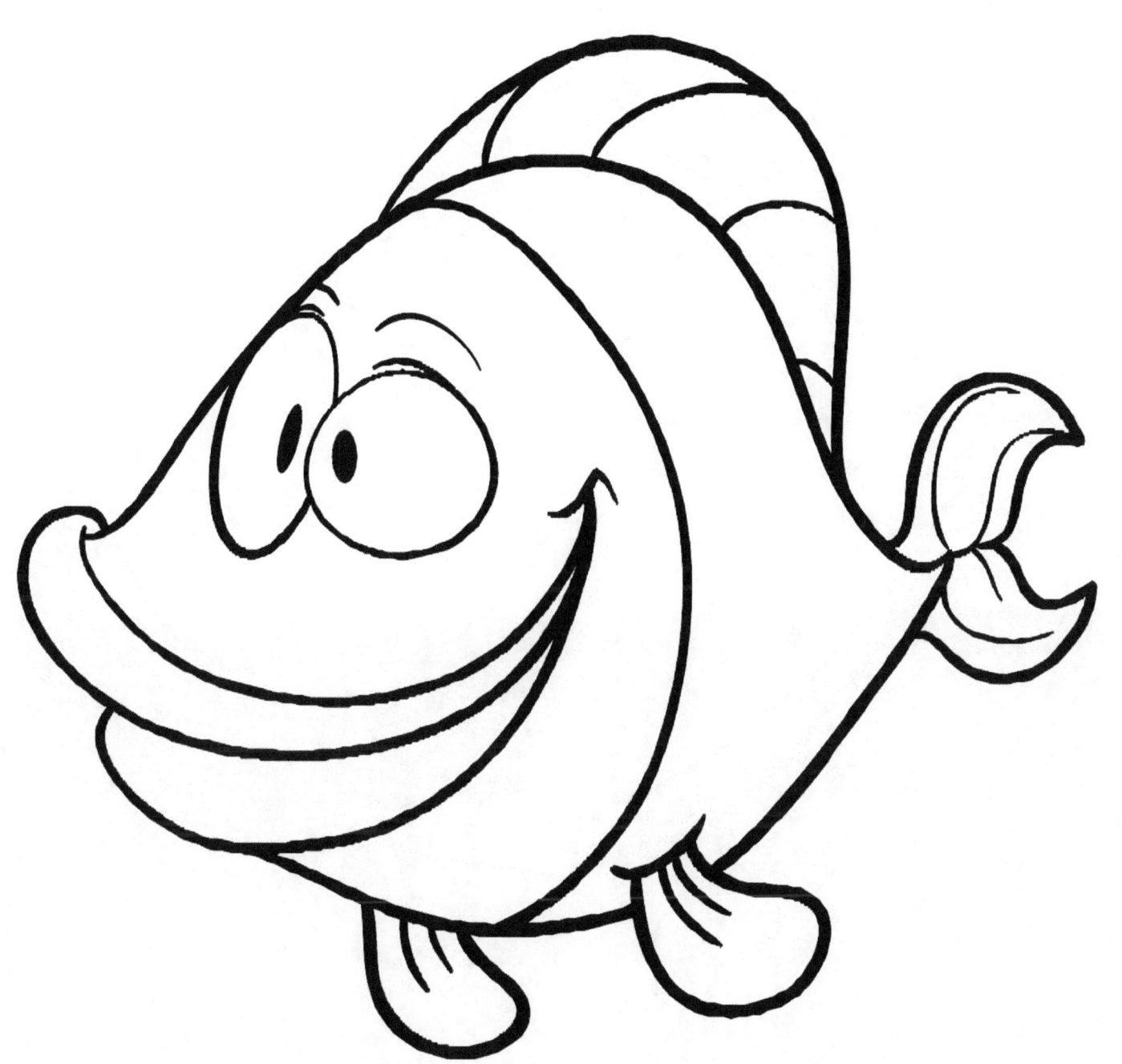

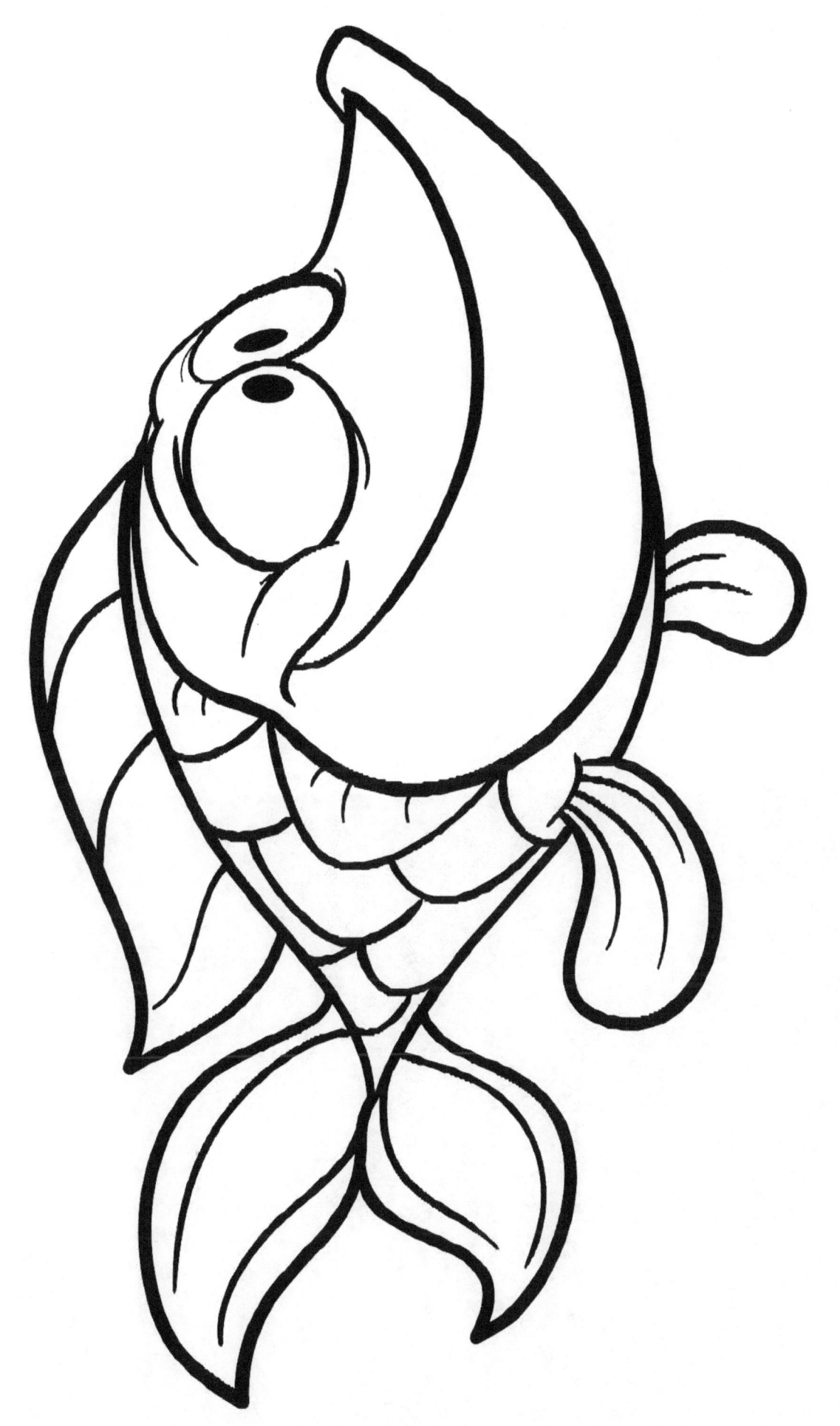

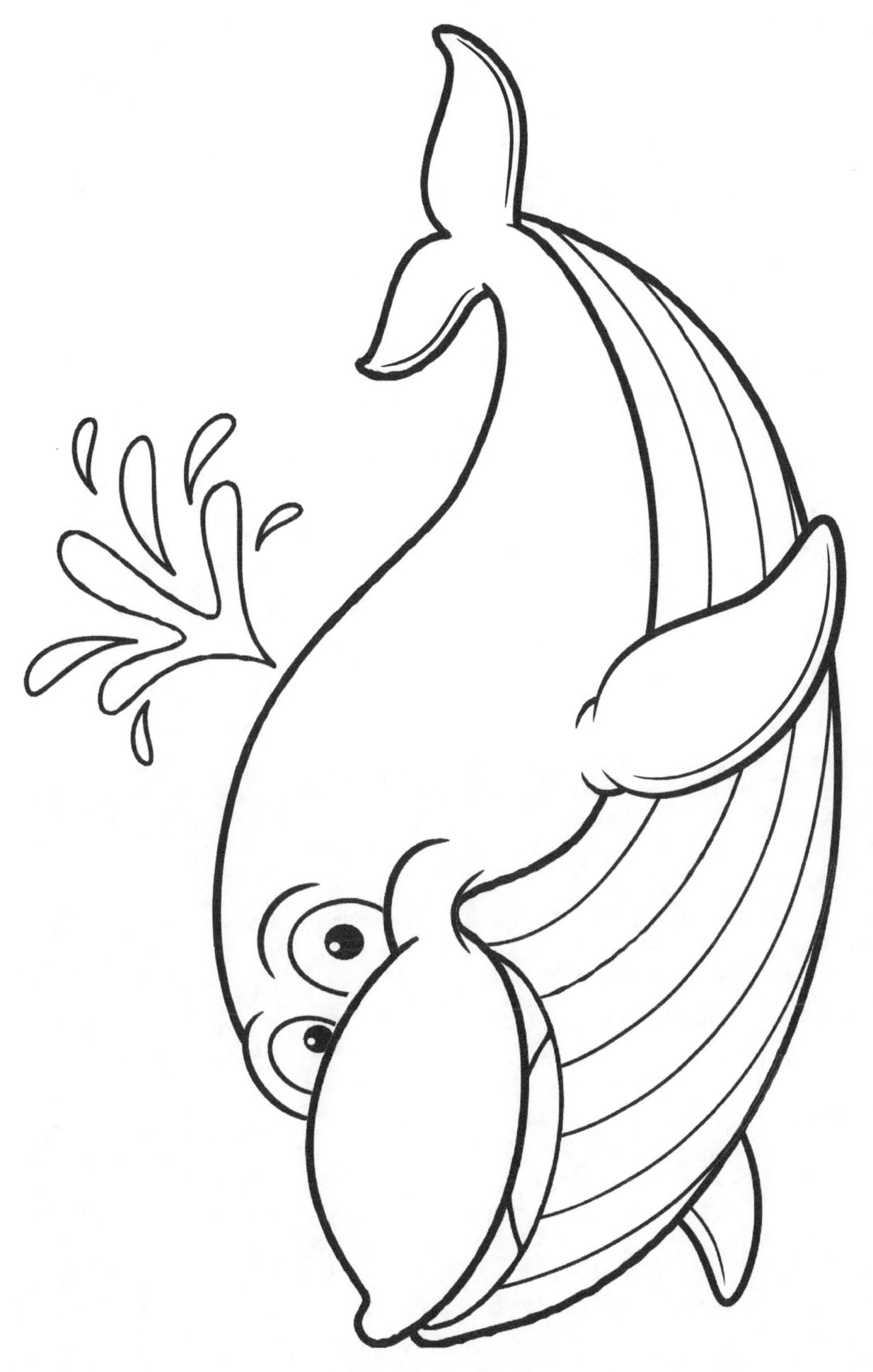

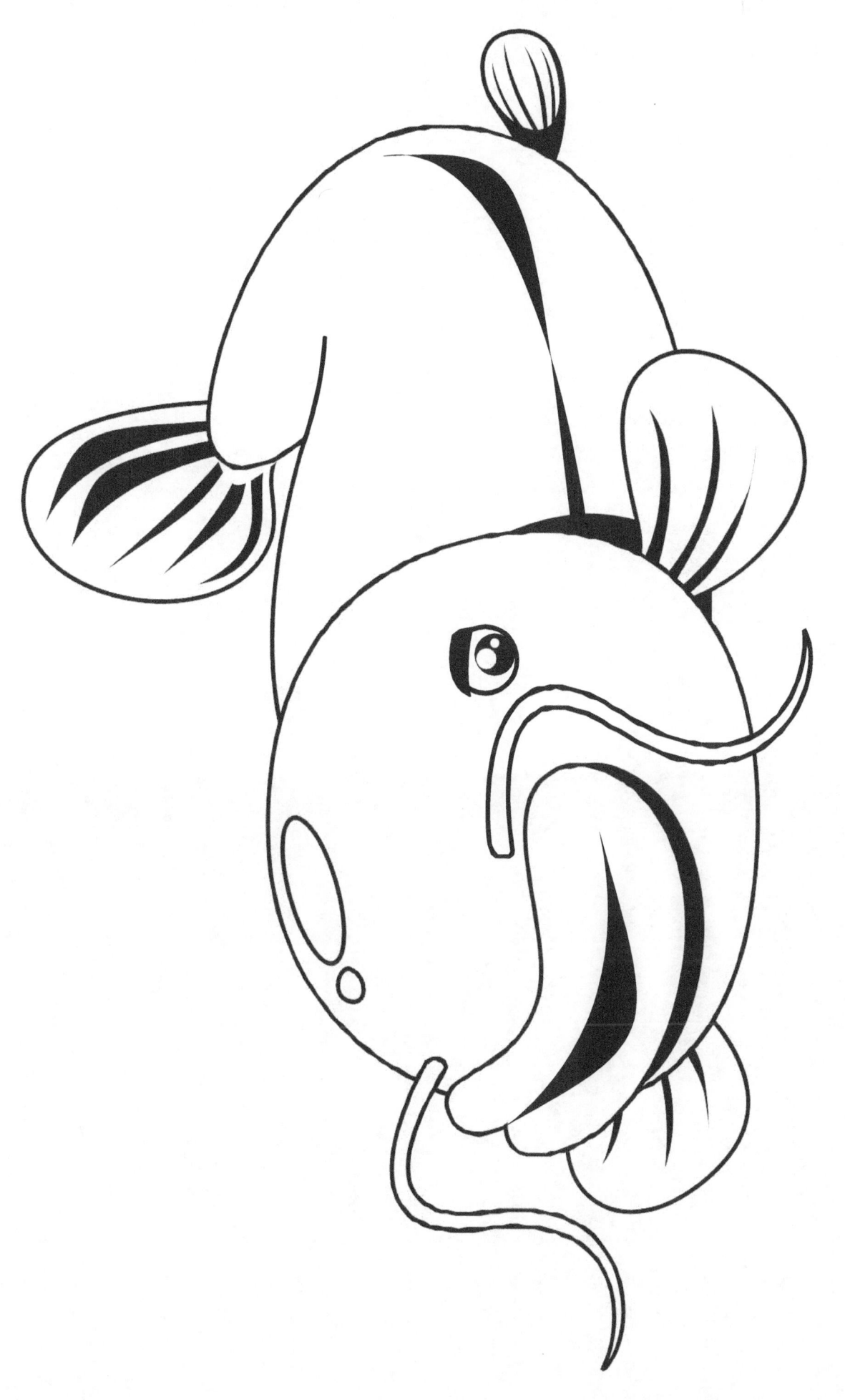

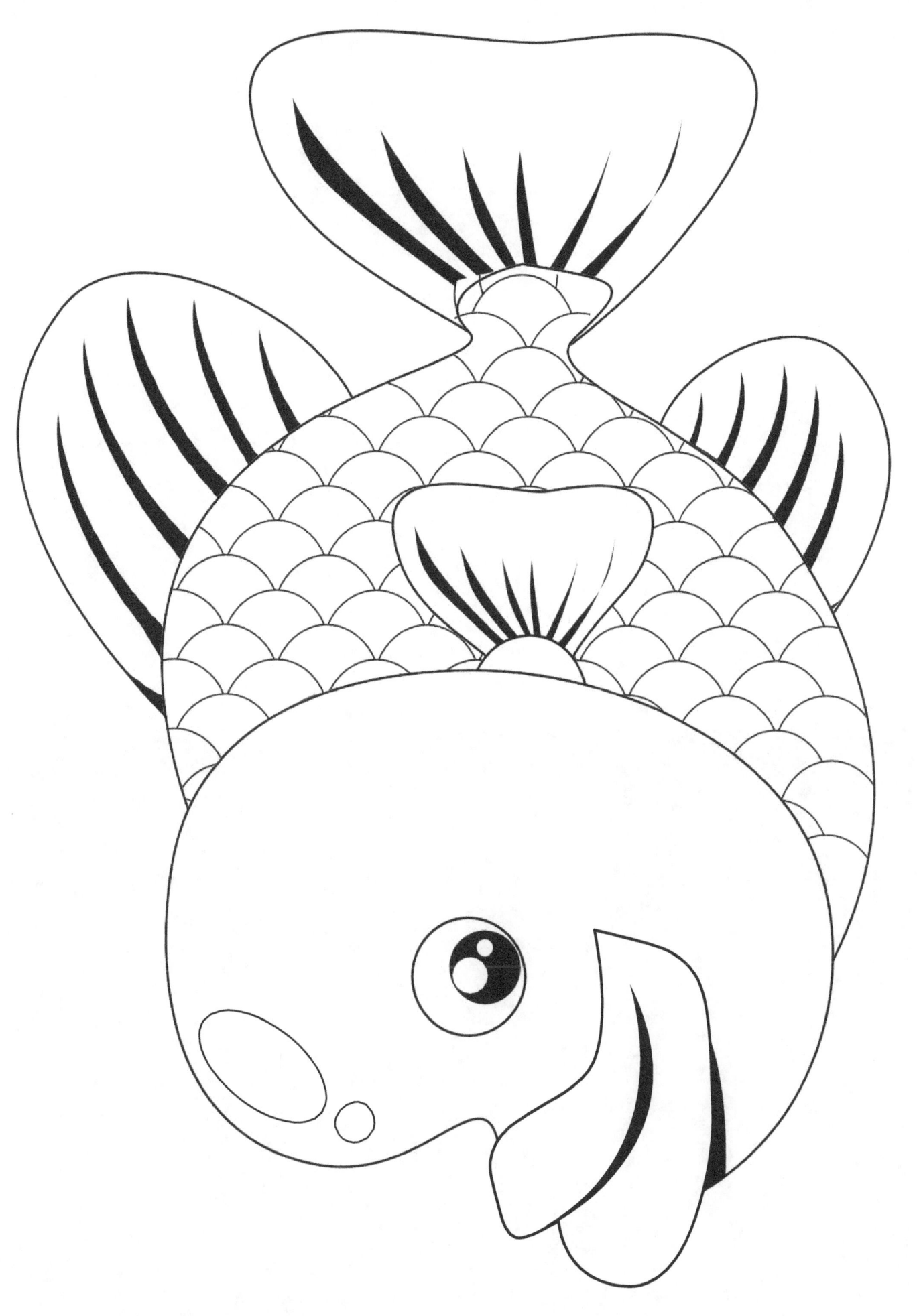

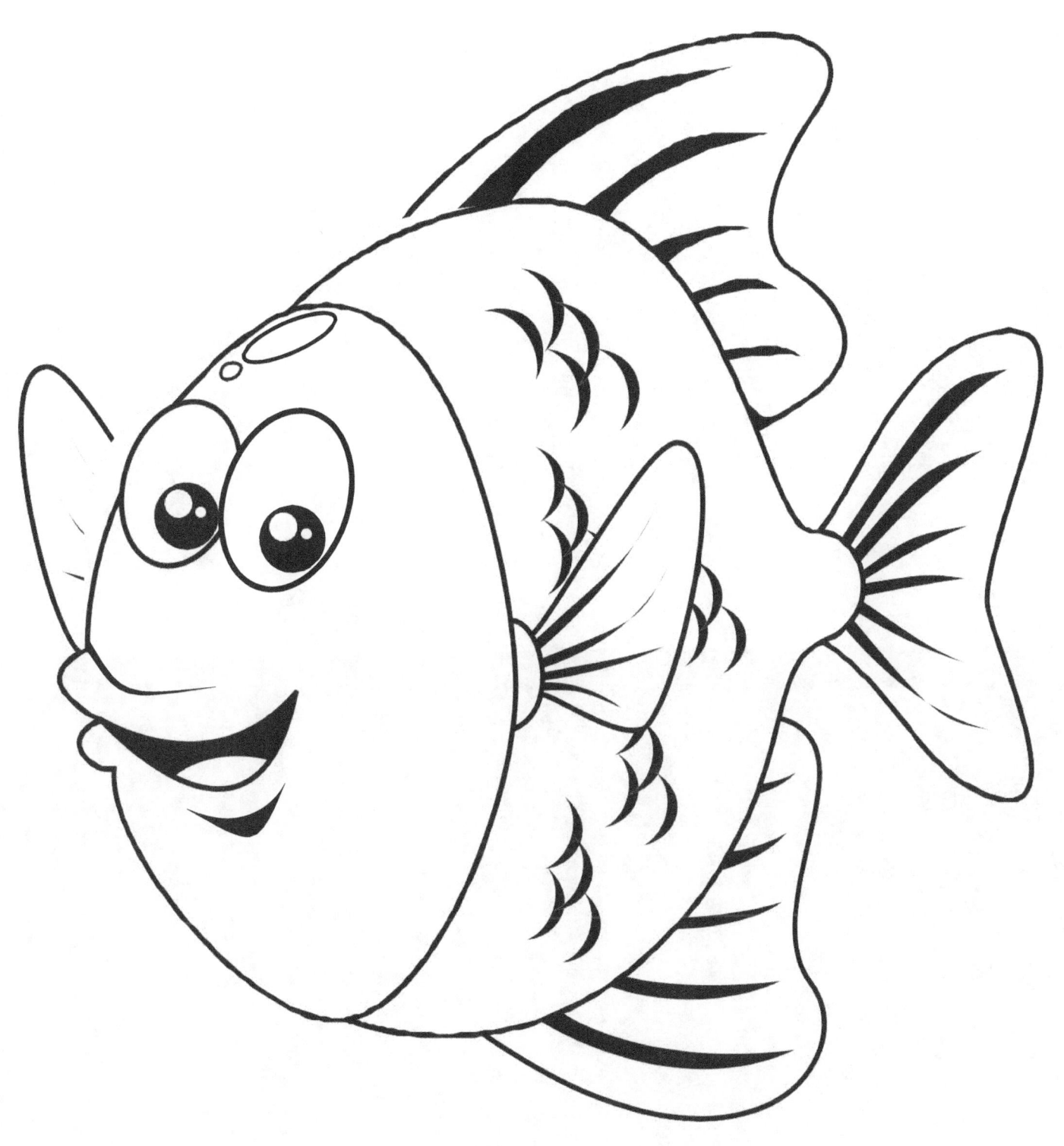

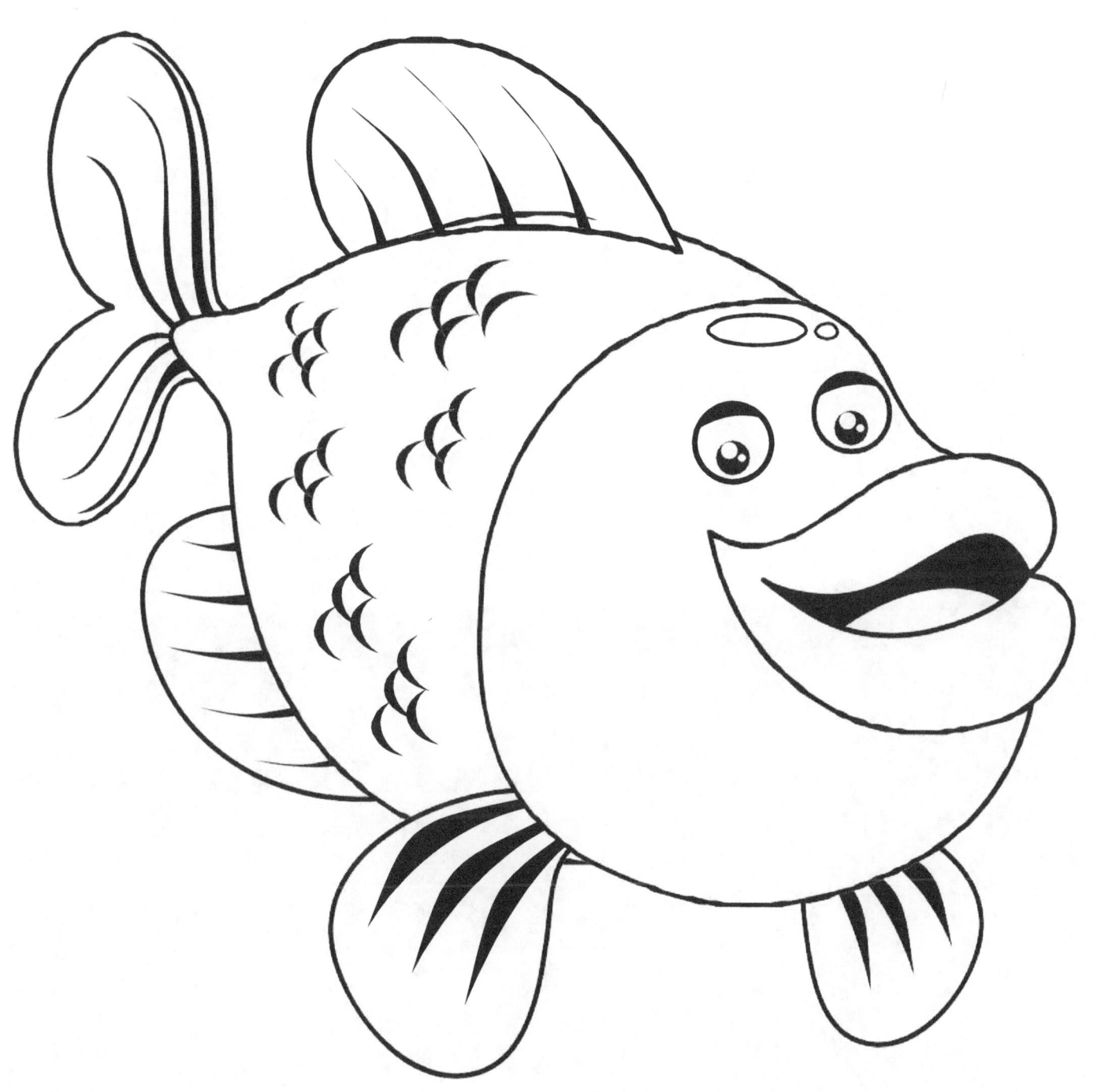

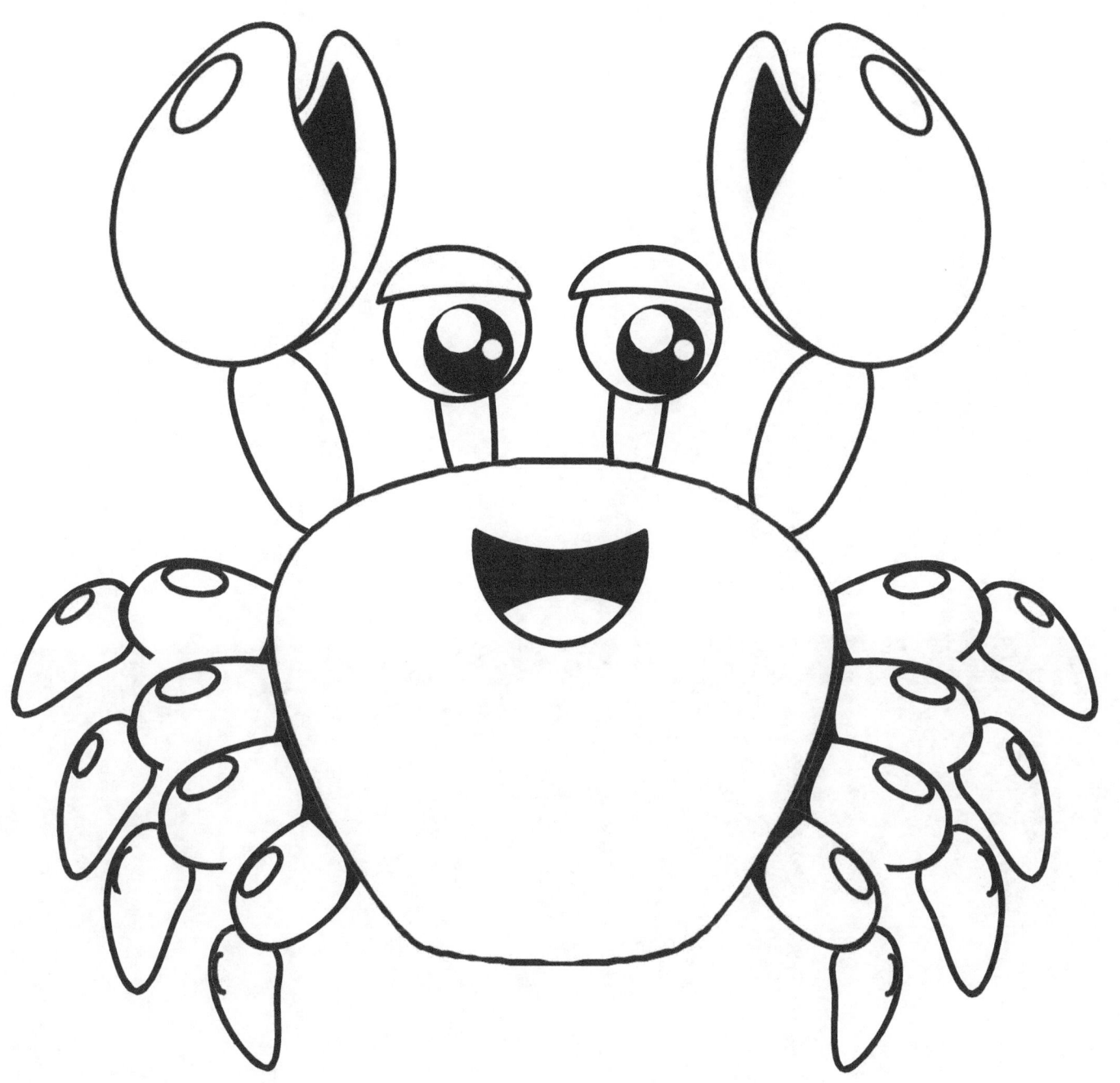

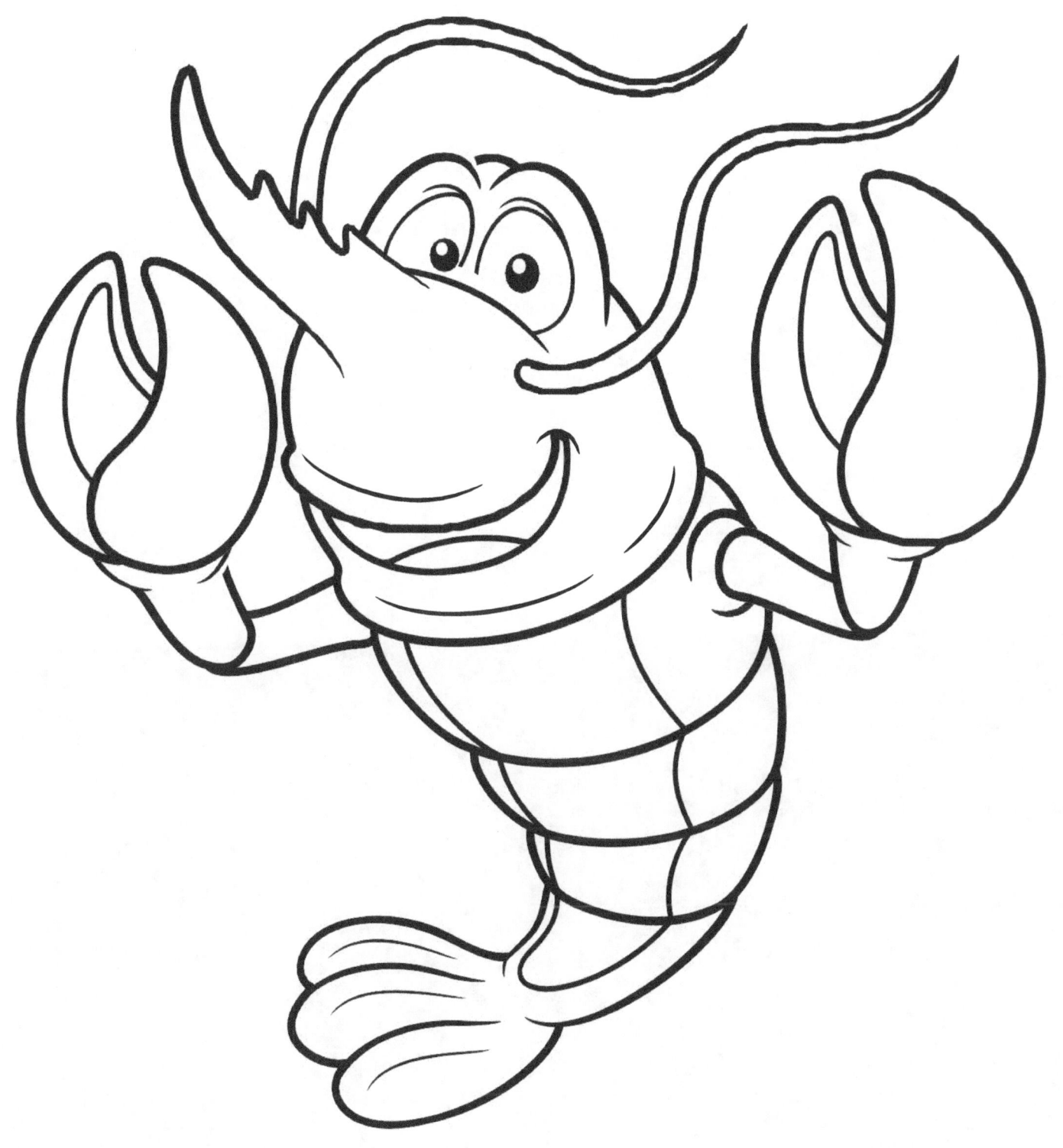

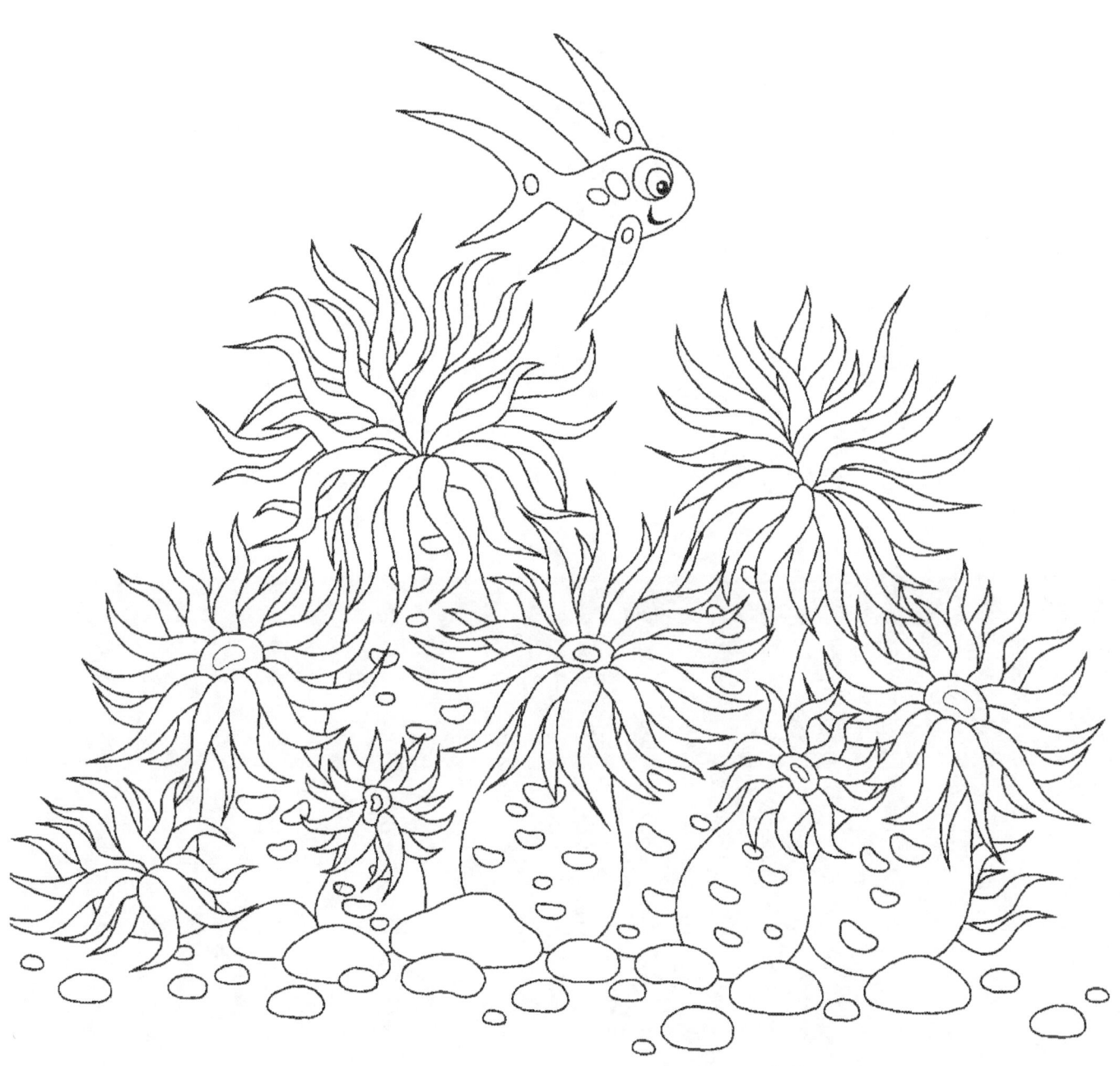

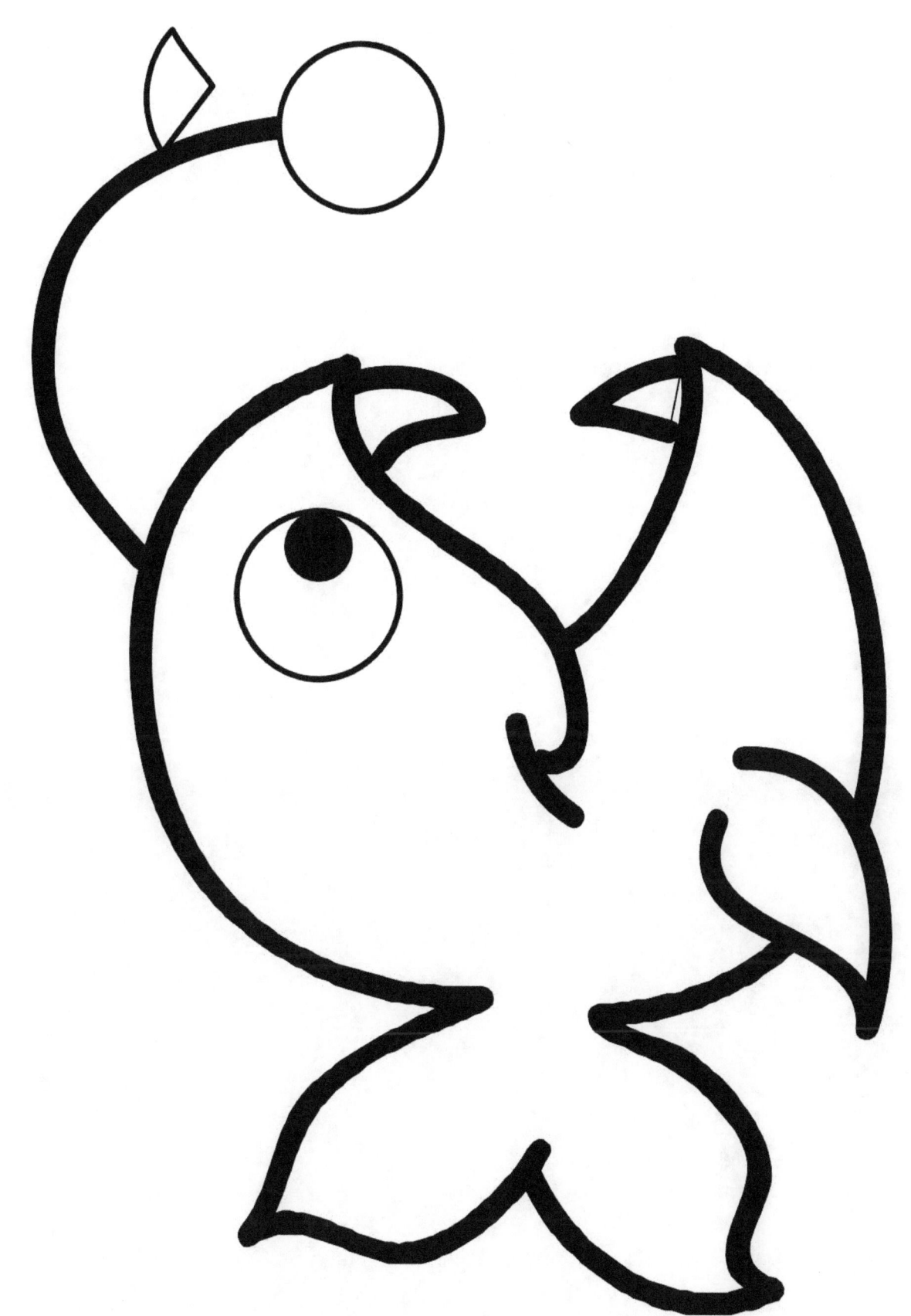

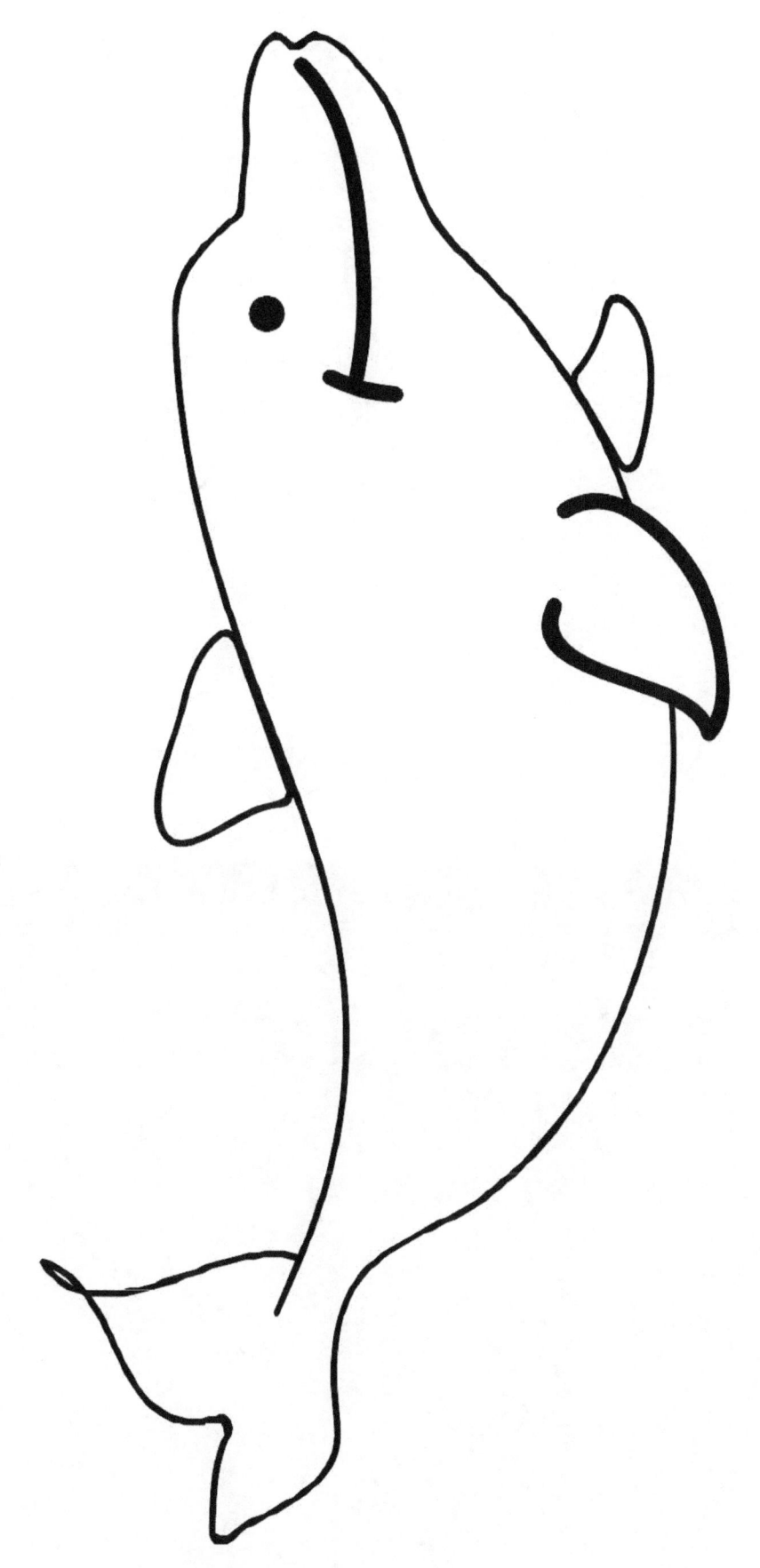

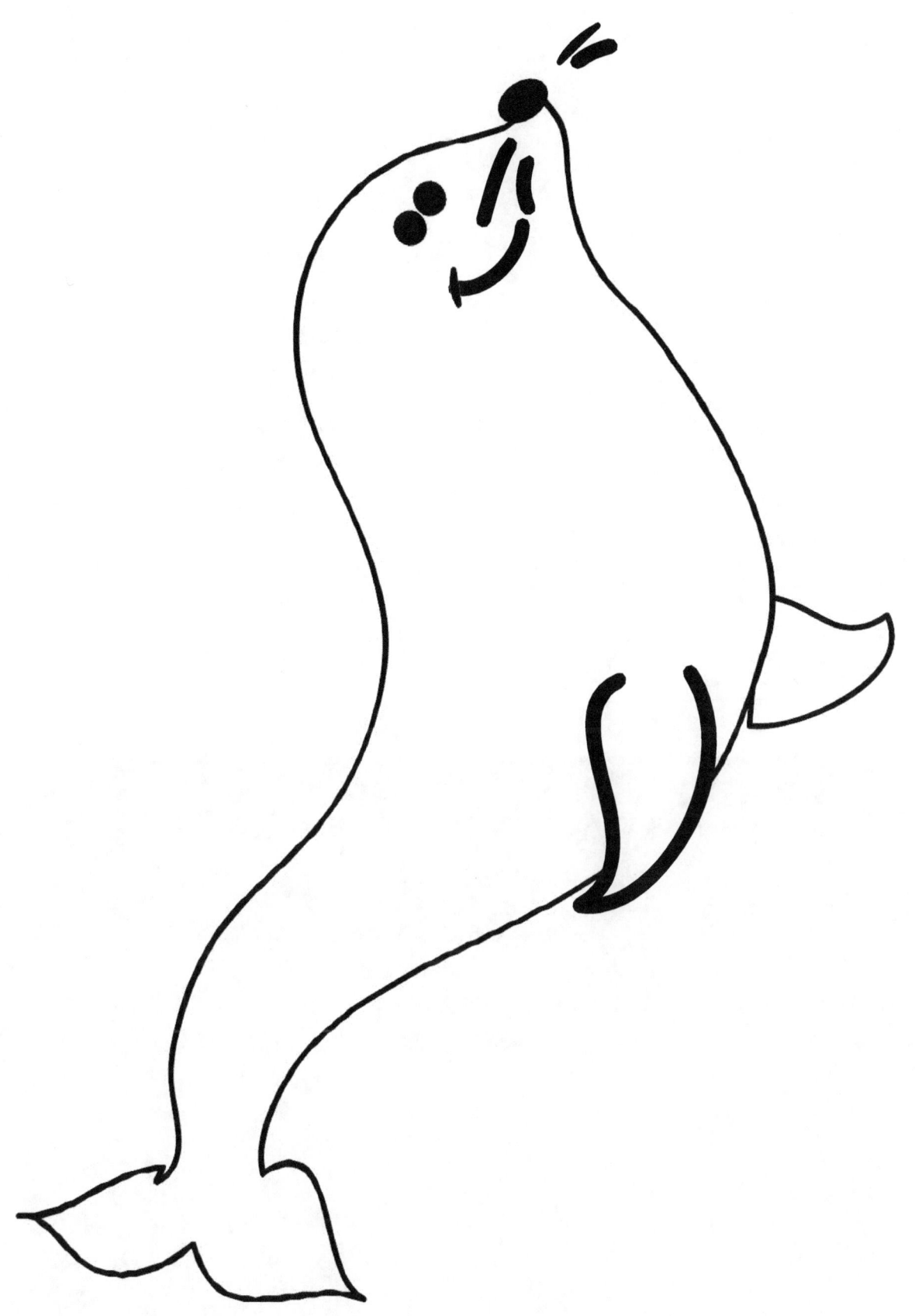

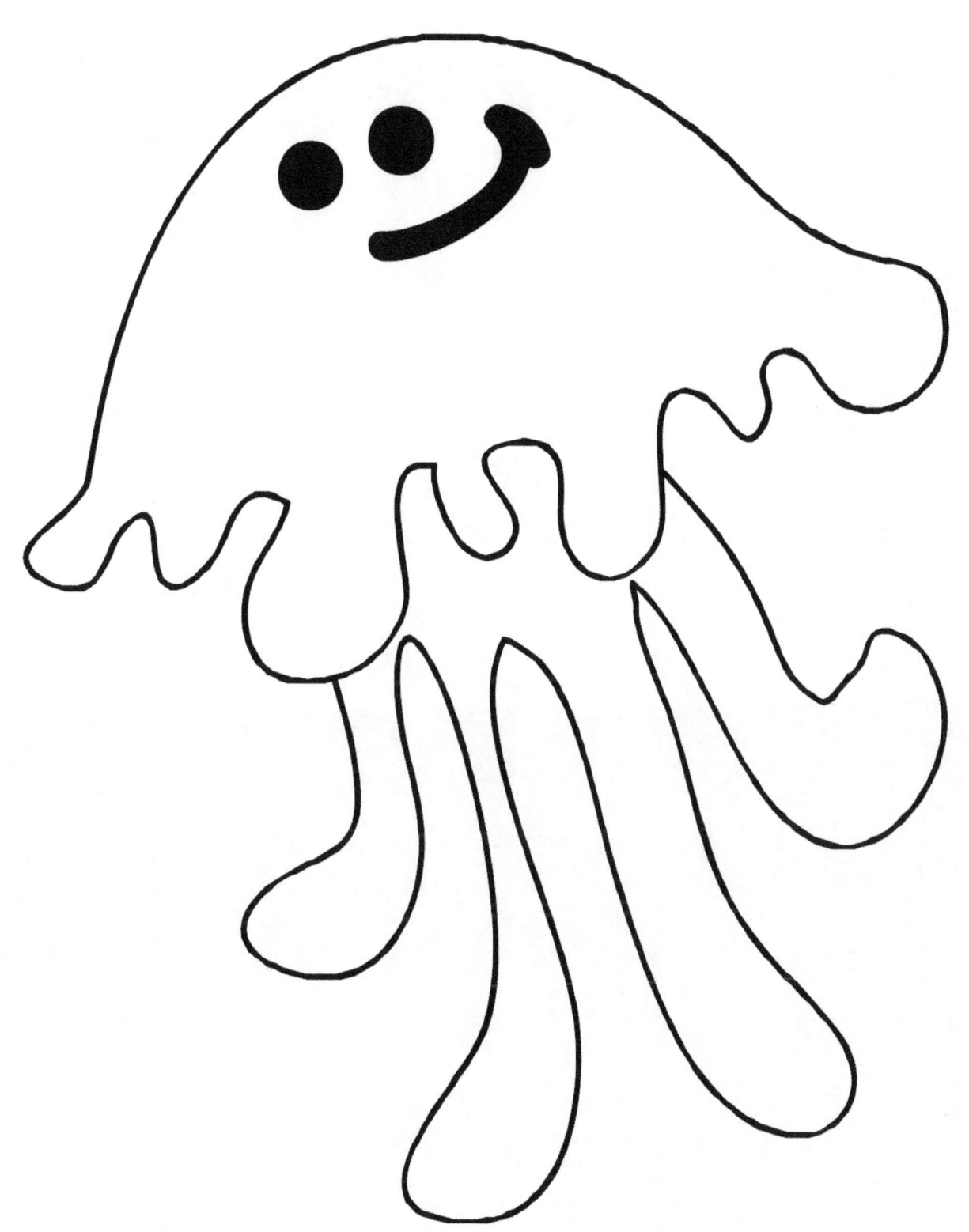

MORE GREAT ARGON MEDIA BOOKS

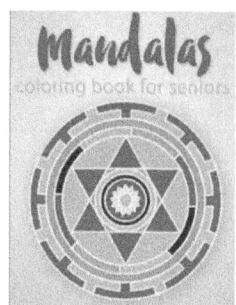

MANDALAS COLORING BOOK for SENIORS

In this uplifting adult coloring book just for Senior Citizens, you will discover the joy and beauty around coloring in these unique mandalas. Mandalas have a mystical quality about their designs. You will enjoy creating one of kind works of art, that you can give as gifts as you create your own colorful patterns from these centuries old designs. Each and every pattern is packed with the calming, peaceful, stress-reducing power you need today!

Order Online at: https://www.createspace.com/5727680

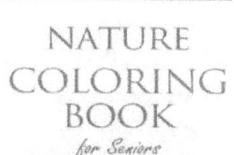

NATURE COLORING BOOK for SENIORS

Every Senior loves nature! Flowers, trees, birds are truly beautiful. Coloring the sights and scenes from nature provides hours of peace, calm and serenity. Inside of Nature Coloring Book for Seniors, you are transported into some of the most beautiful natural scenes ever created. You will lose yourself and track of time as you decide which color and shade works best for your pieces of art. The greatest benefit you'll receive is the pride from completing your work of art.

Order Online at: https://www.createspace.com/5745044

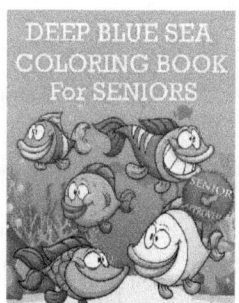

DEEP BLUE SEA COLORING BOOK FOR SENIORS

You can discover an amazing way to grow younger and feel better today!
Every Senior loves the sea and these sea creatures! Color these friendly sea creatures in and bring them to life with every color in the rainbow. Perfect for every grand-parent and senior at every stage or season of life.

The Deep Blue Sea Coloring Book for Seniors is perfect for you to unwind and de-stress your life. It can go with you to the doctor's office, while waiting in line at the pharmacy or while you take your daily coffee break.

Order Online at: https://www.createspace.com/6047940

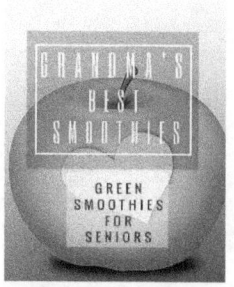

GRANDMA'S BEST SMOOTHIES: Green Smoothies For Seniors

You have worked hard to save up for your retirement. Your health care needs may take all of your savings away. Simply eating green smoothies is one of the best preventative measures you can make towards living long and well as you go through this season of life.

Green Smoothies For Seniors will give you everything you need to start making this small change in your life for the better.

Order Online at: https://www.createspace.com/6047108

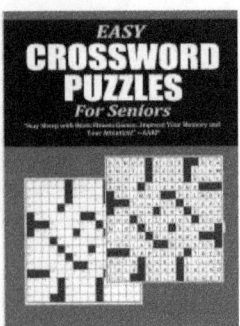

EASY CROSSWORD PUZZLES FOR SENIORS

AARP says, "Stay sharp with brain fitness games...improve memory and your attention!" This is the perfect plan for you if you want to improve and strengthen your mind. It starts with mental exercises you can complete easily every day.

1 – start by ordering this manual
2 - take to using it for just 30 minutes daily
3 – enjoy your new found mental strength

Order Online at: https://www.createspace.com/5708683

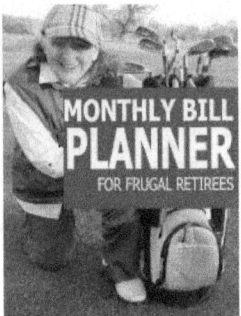

MONTHLY BILL PLANNER FOR FRUGAL RETIREES

You have worked hard your entire life to get to this season of retirement. Planning your finances is more important now than ever. Knowing what is coming in and what goes out is easy with this personalized monthly bill planner. By using this unique planner, you will be able to have more confidence, and control over your money, which frees up resources to splurge on yourself or your grand-children.

Order Online at: https://www.createspace.com/5481058

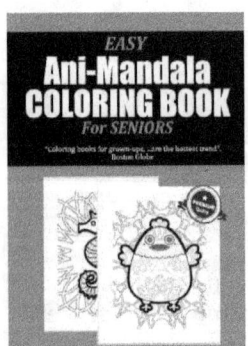

EASY ANI-MANDALA COLORING BOOK FOR SENIORS

Coloring is a one of the most stress-reducing activities you can do. You will love coloring in these custom created animals with a mandala type theme. Every drawing is designed on one page. There is a bleed sheet placed in between each page to protect your art work from gel pen leaking through. This is a perfect gift for someone you love or get one for yourself. Hours of fun and relaxation await you!

Order Online at: https://www.createspace.com/5995541

To learn more about Argon Media resources and to get bonus booklets and gifts, visit our website:

www.ArgonMedia.com

ArgonMediaLLC
Digital Media Guaranteed

Argon Media, LLC
GRAND RAPIDS, MICHIGAN
